Embracing the MonSter
Within:

10 Strategies on Navigating a Chronic Illness through Strength and Perseverance

Kinyotta Johnson

Table of Contents

Dedication

I would like to dedicate this primarily to the woman who was highly influential in my life, my grandmother Idella Louise Hale Winston. Without her I do not know who I would be today. She was a woman who loved me unconditionally, showed compassion, discipline, grace, understanding, and provided me with the nurturing and security I needed through my life. She welcomed anyone she encountered with love, gave the best advice, and loved to have fun. She was the epitome of strength and reason and did not let anybody tell her what to do. I deeply miss her every day and I know she is my guardian angel, smiling down, pushing me to be more, and to do more, to reach others just like me. I miss you and I love you. Until we meet again, "It's never goodbye, it's BE SWEET!"

Secondly, I'd also like to dedicate this to the strongest MS Warrior I have ever met, Aurita Prince Caldwell. A Multiple Sclerosis Warrior herself, to watch her go through the same struggles as me, was difficult. She was the true definition of a woman, a person, which showed perseverance and strength each day. The disease progressed quickly for her. It was her endurance, positive attitude, and her willingness to get up and do what she needed to do, to maintain as much independence as she could hold on to, that truly captivated me. Her choice to show up for herself, her family, and face the day's struggles, with a smile, despite challenges, motivated me more than she'll ever know. She fought this MonSter for 10 years so hard, and left a lasting impression, but God said it was time to rest. Her absence in this world has left a void no one can fill. Watching her fight this incurable disease, while fighting my own battle, is what got me through some days. She encouraged me to go to informational meetings, groups, research, and helped strengthen my hope of beating this disease. Oftentimes we had to laugh through the pain.

I love you both and miss you every day. I am grateful that I can still feel your presence in my life, and I thank you for the time I was blessed to spend with you!

Acknowledgments

I would like to take some time out to thank people that made an impact on my life. First and foremost, I would like to thank my Lord and Savior Jesus Christ for being with me every step of the way even in those dark times. God placed people in my life he knew I would need to get me to the point that I am at now and for that I am truly blessed!

I have met some amazing people along my journey, and I am so thankful that we crossed paths. Through trials and tribulations, you have played pivotal roles in my development throughout the years, and I am forever grateful and love you for that. I am a better human being for knowing you all. I've always agreed that we don't get to choose the families that we are born into, but we do get to choose the family that we experience life with, and I am so blessed to have. From the deepest part of my heart thank you!

My Truman crew:
Weslyn Caldwell you are a force meant to change the world. Never lose that welcoming spirit, you deserve all that is good in this world. Through you, I became part of a family I didn't know I needed and met some of the greatest people by default of knowing you. I have always enjoyed and loved being around the

Embracing the MonSter Within

Caldwell Clan: LaTisha, Carnisha, Keith (I guess HAHA), Courtnei, Xavier, Aurita, Dr. Caldwell, Joe Crowell (you're still my favorite), Carmen, Monique, Ryane, Tahaun, Sheila, Jaylen, Genelle, lil Keith, and the rest of the family, it's so many LOL. Your presence in my life means more than you know. I just hate y'all banned me from playing the saranwrap game one year because I was winning too much LOL. Weslyn always remember: Hugs are Healing to those that want them! You know I love you!

Pinky Nicole Murphy girl you light up any room you walk into and to this day I still don't remember how we met at Truman, but none of that matters because you too introduced me to love and a family that treated me like one of their own, the Murphy Clan: Papa Ronnie, Mama Donna, Dawn, Candace, Sydney, Angel, and Rebekah. Pinky, I love you dearly. Continue to shine brightly my friend, the one who knows everything and if she doesn't know she is going to find out for you.

Toyia Poole girl I am so thankful for you. Your heart is pure in this world of chaos, and I appreciate all that you are. I'm so glad JC Penny brought you to my city and all the time we've shared. You have truly been my calm in the storm of life. Love you to pieces and I want nothing but love and happiness for you. Dennis, take care of my friend, you are just as pure as she is and

I'm so happy you both can share your lives together. Love you both!

I thank my mother for giving birth to me. God chose you as the vessel to bring me into this world and for that I love and thank you. I say thank God for aunts and uncles. Uncle Roney and Aunt Pat I am forever grateful for your generosity and being there for me at one of the most difficult times, I love you more than you could ever know. Aunt Betty and Aunt Joy, your love and support has gotten me through some tough times, you truly are earth's angels, and I could not ask for anything more.

Balaski Family, Tenika, Ryan, McKenna (Kenna Ken), and Mason aka Bubs, y'all are the real MVPs. Thank you so much for just being you. Your ability to have compassion and an open heart to those in need is something the world needs more of and I am grateful to call you family. Your presence adds value to my life. I know if something were to happen to me, Bubs would send out a search party lol. I love y'all.

My Johnson Johnsons Latricia, Jeremy, and Treasure I just love the family you have created, and I cherish that for you. Thank you for supporting and encouraging me. Latricia, inviting me on this spiritual journey at the beginning of this year, provided me with the courage to write this book. Continue to be you. I love y'all.

My Disney Peeps:

Annette, Cletra, Dorrell, Jennie, Marcus, Makini, Mesha, Michael, if it wasn't for Toyia telling me to go to the informational meeting Disney was having on Truman's campus, I would've never met lifelong brothers and sisters from different walks of life. We went through a lot in the fall semester of '01. We had so much fun, including turning 21 that year. Going through 9/11, marriages, kids, illness, life's ups and downs and 24 years later we're still here. I can't imagine life without you in it. It was a blessing in disguise. Even got some extra family, Angelia and Jamie. Knowing both of you through Cletra and Marcus has been a bonus, and I love you all just as much as I love them! I see each one of us changing the world in our own way! Oh by the way, Shrek still makes me think of you all!

Cletra, these international trips have been healing my soul. I love you and am grateful to you for showing me what it really is to Live Life to the Fullest!

Annette, our Marco Polo sessions are just the therapy and spiritual healing I've needed throughout the years. My forever Scorpio sister I love you near and far!

Embracing the MonSter Within

My SMMBC/VOD Family:

Darlean Ware oh how I revel in our chance encounter at Procter & Gamble when I moved back to St. Louis in 2004. If it weren't for you inviting me to Southern Mission Missionary Baptist Church, I would have never found my forever spiritual home, across the water, nonetheless. I can't begin to explain the blessing you and your family: Mama Annie, Darrell, Nate, Sigourney, and lil Nate, have been to me. Thank you for your generosity, advice, love, and continued support no matter what. I love you all!

VOD brought a melodic tune to my desire to grow closer to God. I knew the first time I heard the choir singing I wanted to be a part of it. Willard, John, Kiara, Auqila, Wes, Stephanie, Samara, Sheritha, Tammy, Adrian, Ceci, Erika, Tawanda and so many others within the choir opened their arms and welcomed me like I had been a member for years. I've cherished every moment. Even though I haven't participated in the choir in years I am so happy y'all still think of me and include me. I love you all.

My Stuckey girls have opened my eyes to what dedication to family really means. Your family unit showcases just how sticking together can get you through the toughest times. Kiara, you and Mama Linda are forces to be reckoned with and are providing great examples of strong women Karleigh can look up to. Kiara, you deserve the best in life, and the world needs more of you. Your Daddy would be proud! You are amazing and I love you and all the Stuckey ladies.

John, what can I say to "My Boo" for life. Our candid conversations, real, raw, unfiltered, are exactly what's been needed to help us grow as individuals. I appreciate our bond and friendship, and I wouldn't trade that for anything. You know I love you!

Willard your testimony alone is enough to make someone shout. I am truly humbled to see how far God has brought you through your own struggles. He is not finished yet. You inspire me to keep going and show what a living miracle looks like. Thank you for living your life with Faith, Strength, and Perseverance so others can also see that He is a way maker!

Antonio St. James, you opened my eyes to a whole new perspective on how to heal your body in the most unconventional way. To hear how you overcame and put movement into action because you wanted to survive was just what I needed when you invited me to the Cahokia Mounds for an exercise session. MAN did that first encounter on those steps almost take me out! Your encouragement and help gave me the courage to do something I'd never done or even thought about. My first time making it to the top was such a breathtaking scene. To be on top and to see a 360 view of St. Louis/East St. Louis/Cahokia, was just the motivation I needed to keep moving forward. I feel closer to God when I am up there. I miss those early morning workouts in the mist, among the deer. I thank you and Ceci for showing me that I don't have to do the same thing that everyone does, but that I can find my own way of accomplishing a goal and in my own time. Continue to make your mark on this world. THANK YOU!

Pastor Jerome Jackson 1st Sr. your unwavering love and support will always be remembered. Your style and the way God spoke to me through you is what pushed me to keep fighting when this disease first started to show its face in my life. My relationship with the Most High is because of you and your leadership in SMMBC. I am forever grateful for the impact you have had on my life. You and Mama Jackson's encouragement, candor, love, and Mama Jackson's hugs are the elements I've needed as a reminder that there is something greater to me. I will always hold on to "No Matter Who You Are, Where You've Been, Or What You've Done, God Loves You!"

My DMH peeps:
Paris (Babi) Henderson. You are God's earthly angel. I can't believe how close we have become in these 20 years. We have shared some of life's hardest challenges together. You inspire me daily with your strength and unwavering love for others. You

sacrifice your own wellbeing for the sake of others. Even through your own struggles, you try to maintain a positive attitude, and no one knows the things you've had to endure. I know Mama Taffi is smiling down and putting in a good word with the Lord above. Like you always say, "What's understood doesn't need to be explained." I love you and would do anything for you. Our friendship, sisterhood, is one of the few good things that came out of us working together. I'm so glad God saw fit for our paths to cross. I love you and the world is better because you are in it!

Nicholas Stevens, my Buddy for life. Who would've thought from our initial encounter that we would've grown as close as we did. You know I didn't like you, but God said don't always trust first impressions. Your love and support through sickness and all means the world to me. Although life has sent us in separate directions, I wish nothing but the best in life for you. Thank you for being a part of my life!

Shavonna, Beth, Andrea, Nicole, and Juanequa, you are all phenomenal women, and your presence has enriched my life and the lives of those we encounter. Our friendship is a blessing. We continue to support and motivate one another and all that we do. I know life happens, and we must schedule time to catch up, but the time we do spend with each other is more valuable than you know. I love you all!

My AIL peeps:
Aaron, Courtney, Thomas, Julian, and Katie (my bonus), looking back, that wasn't the best career move I must admit, however, I go where God tells me to go. At the time, I thought a change was needed. To this day, I still cringe at some of the things endured but I digress. There were also some great moments as well, so not all was lost. Everything happens for a reason. I'm glad to have gotten through it. The highlights were meeting all of you which made it all worth it. I love you all and want nothing but blessings and happiness for you!

Laura Breitenstein, my oldest friend. Honey, I love you to the moon and back. Meeting you in high school was meant to be. You are an amazing woman, mother, daughter, sister, aunt, and educator. You take on so many roles without fail. I am lucky to have met you. Your heart is pure and your unwavering ability to help others is just what the SLPS needs. God is guiding your steps, and I know the best is yet to come. Continue to keep your head up and be the compassionate woman that you are. I love you and yes, we need to get together more!

My Book club crew:

Nick Barton, the book club you envisioned brought people together from all walks of life. I'm so honored to have met all its participants and the bonds that were formed outside of the group. It was purpose driven to make us better humans and helped promote success. With the facilitation of Hunter Raburn, and you, I am so thankful for the new literature the book club introduced into my life. The book topics we dissected and discussed, showed various perspectives, and encouraged us to think outside the box. Nick, the growth I've witnessed in you is exceptional and you are destined for greatness. I thank you for just being you. I am proud of the man you are and proud to know you. You are a real example of someone that keeps mastering everything they put their mind to. I look forward to your next idea! While going on my own writing journey, the information I learned from some of the books mentioned and read enlightened me to the impact good book can have on someone's life. This encouraged me to want to share my story to help encourage others. I truly believe nothing happens by chance and God's intention for us to cross paths long ago was much more than I could have ever imagined. God's timing is not a coincidence.

Foreword

It is often said that "Health is Wealth," but what is a person to do once life makes a withdrawal from the health account? How does one continue on then? What is to be done when your Independence now needs assistance? What do you do when you're at the mercy of others?

I met Kinyotta Johnson in church approximately two decades ago. I was intrigued by her quiet patience, her zeal to learn, and room brightening demeanor. She was perceived as a nice, caring individual by her first impression. She continues to be that and more through the present day. A genuine individual that longs for the better good of her fellow human.

I witnessed Kinyotta's battle with an autoimmune disease that began to alter her life, but something about her began to amaze me even more. Although I didn't see her daily, whenever I saw her, she still had a radiance about her. She continued to have the zeal to live her best life. I was amazed when she continued to further her degrees. I was astounded as she pursued and managed new career choices. I was astonished as she became a world traveler, going to places others only dreamed of going. These observances, unbeknownst to me, would be the very motivation to help me through my own challenge with health withdrawals.

In Embracing the MonSter Within: 10 Strategies on Navigating a Chronic Illness through Strength and Perseverance, Kinyotta Johnson shares the hard grasp of what it takes to go through acceptance and adjustment when it comes to major ground shaking changes with health and life challenges. She is extremely knowledgeable of the mental and physical mindset needed to live life to the fullest despite health challenges. She is a veteran when it comes to relinquishing independence and yielding to the kindness of others while maintaining poise, dignity, and grace.

When life makes that heavy withdrawal from health, and you have no idea of how to move on with what will happen next, Embracing the MonSter Within: 10 Strategies on Navigating a Chronic Illness through Strength and Perseverance will help immensely. Kinyotta Johnson has a way of making life changes clear and understandable to those who find themselves in this new and vulnerable situation. She is like a close friend taking your hand, while speaking truth to your soul, as she guides you through a journey she herself has walked.

Will Owens,
Educator/Program Coordinator/Musician/Chronic Health Survivor

Introduction

Dear reader, thank you so much for taking the time to read this book. I wrote this book to let you know that even if you have been diagnosed with a debilitating or chronic illness you can still have a fulfilling life. My name is Kinyotta Johnson, and I have been a Survivor for the last 14 years. When I was first diagnosed with Multiple Sclerosis (MS), I thought my life was over. Multiple sclerosis is a chronic, inflammatory disease of the central nervous system that affects or attacks the myelin sheath of nerve fibers. These attacks are called demyelination and can cause a variety of symptoms. There are primarily four main versions of multiple sclerosis: Clinically isolated syndrome (CIS) which is the first neurological symptom that may be a sign of MS; Relapsing-Remitting (RRMS) where relapses or worsening of symptoms occur but then can go into remission; Secondary Progressive (SPMS) the gradual worsening of RRMS with no clear sign of remission; and Primary Progressive (PPMS) where symptoms become worse, progressing from the very beginning with no relapses or remission.

MS affects everyone differently and there is no cure, only disease modifying therapies (DMT), medications, and/or lifestyle changes, to manage the symptoms. This was a diagnosis I did not want to hear. However, when I took time to pause, reflect, and center myself, I knew that my faith was going to bring me through. By no means am I an expert on all things Multiple Sclerosis, but I am an expert on my journey. So, if you don't mind, I would like to share some of the lessons that I have learned, as I continue learning every day. Even if you cannot relate to battling with a chronic illness, maybe this can help you support a loved one, a friend, a colleague, or even a stranger.

Chapter 1
Accept, Adjust, Adapt

Acceptance means acknowledging reality without resistance or judgment, regardless of whether you like or want the situation. It's about recognizing what's happening and releasing the desire to change it. To adjust can be defined as altering or moving in a slightly different way, to achieve the desired fit. Or it can mean adapting or becoming used to a new situation. Being able to accept, adjust, and adapt to change can be quite scary for many. In life, EVERYDAY, we must choose to embrace change, and with that change, we must develop the strength to persevere. It is important to ACCEPT the situation for what it is, ADJUST the best way that we can, and ADAPT to that new reality. This isn't always easy but it's important to add quality to our lives. It can be hard for people to overcome obstacles in life, because we're so used to routines. We're so used to being able to do things a certain way, say things a certain way, see things a certain way, and when that obstacle comes and hits us right in the face, it knocks our whole world view down. It causes us to take a step back and realize we can't do things the way that we were used to doing. We can't interact with people the way that we used to, we can't do that job the way that we used to, we can't show up for our families the way that we used to, and that can be extremely traumatic. It's so important for you to learn how to ACCEPT the challenges presented to you, ADJUST to how you must navigate now, and ADAPT to your new environment, new schedules, and new routines because the life you once had is no longer available to you.

Let me tell you about a time where I had to ACCEPT, ADJUST, and ADAPT to my situation. I was 30 years old at the time. I was going to school and working full-time. I started noticing numbness in my hands and I didn't think much of it. I just thought, hey I've been typing a lot of papers lately, and I've been working a lot lately, so my hands are just tired. Then that numbness traveled to my feet and I'm like something's not quite right. So, I decided to go to the emergency room. They couldn't tell me anything, so I kept going on with my normal life, working and going to my classes in the evenings. It wasn't getting better. I felt like the symptoms were getting worse, so I went to another emergency room. They also couldn't tell me anything. I had to continue to push through, regardless of my symptoms. After several weeks, it was getting to the point where the numbness in my body was advancing even more, making it more difficult for me to function. I decided to go to another ER. Third time's a charm, right? This time, while laying a bed in that ER, the doctor said to me, "well you're 30 years old and it could be symptoms of Multiple Sclerosis, but they wouldn't know until you have an MRI," then he left the room. No explanation, he just left. Alone, all I could hear were the sounds of machines beeping, people talking, and chaos in the emergency room. I'd never heard anything about Multiple Sclerosis. When he came back in to present my discharge paperwork, I asked him to explain. He said you'd have to see a specialist to confirm. I left that hospital mind wandering to several dark places.

It took me 6 months to get in to see a specialist, a neurologist, and by that time my entire body was almost completely numb, which I found out later is called an MS Hug. Mind you, I still went to work, to school, and spent time with family and friends, even though it was becoming increasingly difficult for me to function. It was difficult for me to walk, use my hands, and my legs. When I was finally able to get in to see the neurologist, he scheduled the MRI immediately. It was my first time ever in this tube of a machine with loud sounds everywhere. By the time my friend took me home, because I could not drive myself there and back, I received a phone call later that night from the neurologist who informed me that I needed to be in the hospital right away. Of course, this created a panic like no other I had ever experienced. My heart was racing, anxiety set in. I could not gather my thoughts. All I could say to him is that my ride's not here, I can't drive myself. He said I'm going to make sure you have a hospital room waiting for you tomorrow morning. It should only be a 3-day hospital stay to get some more tests and treat you with IV steroids to help increase your strength. I agreed. The next morning, my friend came to pick me up and transported me to the hospital. They admitted me and he told me the MRI I had that Friday night showed lesions on my brain and spine. I was told that this is usually a symptom, or a sign, of Multiple Sclerosis but they wouldn't be able to tell for sure until they did a lumbar puncture, commonly called a spinal tap. He started me on IV steroids for my 3-day hospital admission. The spinal tap would be able to rule out whether it's meningitis or multiple sclerosis.

A series of unfortunate events occurred. I went to have a spinal tap. Then, there was a hospital shut down. Why? It was tornado season and there was severe weather, producing tornadoes here in the Midwest. The hospital was shut down for people to shelter in place. I was on the operating table for 4 hours with a needle in my back, and they could not get any spinal fluid, so they sent me back up to my room. They opened the hospital back allowing visitors. The doctor said they were going to try again tomorrow. I was so grateful to see that once the hospital was reopened, I had friends and family waiting on me. I was instructed after my spinal tap, I had to lay flat on my back, for 6-8 hours. I'm a reader and love music so to receive a new book to occupy my time was the best. Just having someone there to distract me from the current situation was healing for me. The next day, a second spinal tap produced enough spinal fluid to be tested. Test results confirmed it was Multiple Sclerosis. Unfortunately, right after that procedure, I developed a horrible headache. Headache is a sign of spinal fluid leakage. To treat the headache, they explained doing a procedure called a blood patch. A blood patch is them taking your blood and inserting it into your spine, to stop the spinal fluid leakage. Once that was completed, I felt immediate relief and was transported back up to my hospital room. I went to the bathroom and came out to wash my hands at the sink. I remember standing by the sink and I felt strange, an Aura, (I found out later that's what it is called). I remember yelling for help and then I blacked out. When I woke up, the nurses told me, as they were coming into my room, I was having a seizure. I had what's called a Grand Mal seizure. During that seizure, I hit my head on the floor, which caused a brain bleed or subdural hematoma, which is the medical term. After scans, they saw that, not only did I have a brain bleed, two blood clots had formed and traveled to my brain, pressing on my venous sinus thrombosis, affecting my vision. These blood clots are what caused my seizure. I could not see straight because of the build of pressure on my brain. My doctors did not know what to do. They could not give me medication because each medication for each problem would contradict one another and make the problem worse. All I could do was wait and pray. I was told, if it didn't get better they would have to do brain surgery to reduce the swelling. It was a waiting game for me. I was in and out of ICU and my doctors told me that they had to do research on my particular situation. I spent one week in Christian Northeast Hospital then transferred over Memorial Day weekend to Barnes Hospital.

A 3-day hospital stay turned into a true nightmare. Fifteen days later, I was finally discharged. During the longest and scariest 15 days of my life, I had a Grand Mal seizure, MS hug, double vision, weak extremities, sprained ankle, low blood count, and a poor immune system. Nurses wheeled me out to the car where my friend was waiting for me. I shuffled as best I could, to the car, with my walker and wearing my eye patch. I left Barnes Hospital looking like a broken down "Slick Rick," as a friend would later call me, with the new reality of Multiple Sclerosis, an incurable disease I knew nothing about. At 30 years old, my entire body just gave out on me. I looked at the doctors and I said: Well, what do I need to do to get better? Being told this is not something that can get better, because the damage has already been done, was hard to grasp. I wasn't happy about any of this. However I had to tell myself, you can learn to ACCEPT, ADJUST, and ADAPT to this new way of life. I had to take the doctor's recommendations, do physical therapy, and listen to the specialists to help me manage my new normal. I still have my walker hidden in the back of a closet as a reminder of what God has brought me through.

Can you imagine being 30 years old thinking you have so much time left, to do what you want in life, only to realize tomorrow is not promised? Once I was finally released from the hospital, and back at home alone, I had some decisions to make. I was either going to let this discourage me or I was going to fight. I decided I was going to fight. I attended my follow-up visits with my neurologist, hematologist, ophthalmologist, primary care, physical therapist, and occupational therapists. Seeing so many specialists was quite overwhelming. During a visit with my neurologist, she says to me "You're a one in a million case. We don't see cases like this, and it is a miracle that you are here!" I was not scared about my situation until that moment. During the entire ordeal, I was thinking, well what do I need to do to get better? Never did I think that I could have died. I remember my pastor praying with me and for me by my bedside while in the ICU. There were also friends and family that came to visit, who I saw crying at my situation. I had to tell them if you're here to cry, I need you to leave because it was just too much to handle at the time. I didn't need to see that. God had other plans for me. He is in the business of making miracles happen. I did the only thing I could do, went to my appointments and listened to what my doctors told me to do, including my physical therapy and occupational therapy. I stayed at home, I was too weak to drive anyway, and I didn't trust my vision. I wore the eye patch over one eye, to correct my vision. Six to 8 weeks later, my symptoms improved. I could walk better, and I could see again. I decided that this was not the end for me, and this is just another challenge that I must ACCEPT, ADJUST, and ADAPT to in my environment, including researching and learning what works for my mind, body, and spirit.

REFLECTION

You have the POWER to learn what works for you. REST is so important. Rest and notify doctors when you feel a change in your body. Let's face it, a lot of people hate going to the doctor so this may not be easy for some. However, the sooner you go, the sooner you can address the problem. It is ok to ask for help, there is no shame in it. Sometimes the best medicine is to talk to someone or write it down. It's almost like purging your mind and body of toxins. Negative self-talk is hazardous to the mind, body, and soul. Talk to a therapist, talk to your pastor, your doctors, your family, and friends. Gaining different perspectives could save your life. I had to utilize my support system. As a person who was so used to doing everything on my own, I want you to realize that you were not put here to be alone and you should never be afraid to ask for help when you need it. You'll be surprised at how many people are willing to help you if you just ask. There's no reason why you must do it all alone. Make sure you have the right people in your corner. With the right support and tools, you will be able to ACCEPT any situation, ADJUST to any circumstance, and ADAPT to your new reality! Not everything will go according to plan so be ready. YOU'VE GOT THIS!

Chapter 2

Know this is Not a Death

Sentence

What is death? According to the Merriam-Webster Dictionary, death is a permanent cessation of all vital functions, it's the end of life. However, there are many different forms of death that people don't acknowledge. Death doesn't have to just be in the physical form. It could be the loss of someone close to you, the loss of a job, the loss of a friendship, the loss of a relationship, or it could be the loss of your identity. What do I mean when I say the loss of your identity? Navigating through life the way you're used to doing. Such as, the way you used to walk, the way you used to talk, the way you used to cook, the way you used to clean, the way you used to bathe, the way you used to see, the way you used to hear, the way you used to feel, just the way that you used to show up in this world has died. It's important to know that just because you receive devastating news, such as being diagnosed with a potentially debilitating disease, that this isn't the end of life for you. Even with this newfound information, just know there is more life for you to live. Death is not something that many people want to talk about, yet it's the only guaranteed thing to happen to every one of us. We choose to avoid the conversation for fear of the unknown, which is completely understandable. No one wants to face their own mortality or believe it's possible they won't be here the next day, the next hour, or even the next minute. However, that is a real possibility. We don't know the day nor the time at which we will have our last breath.

I think back to one day in the hospital, while lying in bed, too weak to go to the bathroom, having this foley catheter to catch my urine but I had to have a bowel movement. I had to wait for assistance from a tech or a nurse to use a bedpan. I couldn't wait. Whether help was there or not, waiting wasn't an option, so I surrendered. Talk about frustration. I was so ashamed of myself. The real embarrassment was when this male nurse walked in to assist. I saw him and thought ooh he's cute too. Why is this happening? I defecated all over the bed and myself, and he would be the one cleaning me up. To my surprise, and relief, he was the gentlest and had the best bedside manner I had experienced.

For the beginning of my journey, being in and out of hospital settings and doctor's offices, being poked, prodded, and scanned was very exhausting. I got to a point where I was just tired of it all. I was tired of seeing doctors. I was tired of getting blood work. I was tired of being scanned, stuck with needles, and test after test. I asked many questions. I reminded myself; this is what I need to do to survive. I am a survivor. I want to continue to be a survivor. I want to fight this autoimmune disorder. It is hard while realizing that my own body is attacking itself, and I had to figure out how to beat it. I remember walking around the grocery store with my walker, wearing my eye patch, and this little boy comes up to me and he asks so cheerfully, "are you a pirate?" All I could do was laugh and the horror on his mother's face was quite comical. I looked down at the little boy and I told him "No I'm not a pirate." He then asked, "is your eye still there?" As his mom was frantically trying to take him away, I said "no I still have my eye, I just need to wear this right now to correct my vision." I lifted the eye patch to show him that my eye was still there. I appreciate his innocence so much. I needed that laugh because it let me know two things. One, I am still alive, and two kids have no filter. They will most certainly bring you back to reality. They find excitement in the smallest things. He genuinely seemed excited when he thought I was a pirate, and that's when I realized this isn't a DEATH SENTENCE. As adults, it's important to preserve some sort of childhood innocence to see the world more clearly. There is plenty of LIFE to LIVE. This is just another obstacle or hurdle I needed to get through. It was also a teaching moment. I had to choose to LIVE, so I acted. I was tired of sitting in the house, waiting for other people to drive me places because my vision still wasn't corrected. I talked to my ophthalmologist who informed me I could have prisms created to put in my glasses, which would semi help me see better until my eyes were strong enough to correct the problem. The prisms worked and I was so grateful because this was one step closer to becoming more independent. I was on track to getting a portion of myself back.

Think of a time when you got some information and you thought that it was going to be the end of the world. How did it make you feel? I'm sure your mind traveled to some dark places. I'm here to tell you, IT'S NOT THE END. The number one, and most important thing you should do, is allow yourself the ability to GRIEVE. BE STILL IN THAT MOMENT. Feel what you feel. If you need to take time alone to process, which is something that I needed to do, please give yourself space to process without others' opinions. Then TAKE ACTION! I cannot stress how much MOVEMENT, no matter how small, is so IMPORTANT. Sometimes venting to a loved one, or someone who has gone through the same thing that you have gone through, is another way to help you manage. Seeking professional help is not something to be ashamed of either. I encourage you to seek help when needed. An outside view on your situation, from someone who does not know you personally, is a way for you to let your guard down without fear of being judged. Remember You Are Not Alone, and you will get through it, but you must GO THROUGH IT TO GET TO THE OTHER SIDE. Becoming better means being PROACTIVE in your own life. Do not let the fear of the unknown DISCOURAGE you.

REFLECTION

As I said in the beginning of this chapter, death and the grief that comes with death, manifests itself in several ways. Losing your sense of self is a form of death not often discussed. Yes, we can grieve the loss of the person we once were, just as if we are grieving the loss of someone who is physically no longer here. We must learn to navigate life, as a new being in a world used to seeing us in one way, yet we can no longer show up as that person. That is ok. Give yourself time, grace, and the willingness to learn how to discover this new you. It's going to be hard at first, but it is possible to overcome that sense of loss. Some ways in taking control of the new you are:

- Exercising (movement is so important)
- Reading a book or magazine, adult coloring books
- Spending time outdoors or traveling
- Journaling

- Listening to music or watching a movie
- Spending time with someone who motivates you, makes you laugh, or calms you
- Speaking to a professional

Whatever you choose, make sure you TAKE ACTION and know this temporary moment is not the END!

Chapter 3

Live Your Life to the Fullest

What is life? What is it to live? Andy Andrews said, "Life itself is a privilege, but to live life to the FULLEST, well that is a choice." To Live in simple terms, is to remain alive. Oftentimes people don't put much living into their everyday life. Most people go about their normal daily routines, wake up, eat breakfast, go to work, take care of the kids, take the kids to school, and come back home to get ready for the next day of this mundane cycle of the same thing. People exist, but they're not actually living, which is a depressing thought. No one should have to wake up every day, which is a God-given act, and dread what lies ahead. A lot of people are so consumed and focused with making sure the bills get paid, making sure the bare necessities are taken care of that, they forget to intentionally take a moment, pause, and appreciate being able to breathe, being able to see, being able to touch, being able to hear, being able to smell, being able to walk, being able to talk, having the ability to go to work, having the ability to take care of their kids, having the ability to do what some wish they could. People do not realize how priceless this is. Life exists in the smallest things. Living in the moment is where we find peace and appreciation for what we already have. The only guarantee we have is NOW. Too many people are worried about the future or consumed with their past, not realizing that the past is gone, which is something you cannot change, and the future is not here. Yes, the past is always present in our memories, but the most vital thing for any of us to do is to appreciate the gift of being in the present and never take that for granted.

I was about 5 years into my diagnosis, still trying to figure out how to navigate life. What works for me and what doesn't. I had a relapse and ended up in the hospital for 3 days for IV steroids, then I was sent home with oral medications. Here I am again, just hoping for the best. Hopefully, the symptoms will clear up, but to this day my hands have been numb. It's like that feeling you get when your hand or foot falls asleep. This is one residual effect that I must deal with including pain and extreme chronic fatigue every day. My energy level is not even half of what a normal person has, but I wake up and I get out and do what I need to do, because nobody is going to do it for me. I choose not to lay in bed and surrender. One day, a dear friend contacted me. We met back in college. We were in an internship at Disney World together. She tells me that one of her closest friends is living in

Panama City Panama and asked me if I wanted to go. I had not traveled and didn't even have a passport, not since I was a child. I had not experienced traveling internationally as an adult. I was quite intrigued, contemplated, and decided I don't know if I'm going to be able to go to another country with my condition. How was I going to be able to function in unknown places? It was a scary thought; however, I knew I didn't want to continue the same boring path. Listening to God, He said to me, you don't have to miss out on opportunities just because you have this diagnosis. After much debate, I told her yeah, I'm game for going. I filled out the application to get my passport, went through the process and was so excited when that passport came in the mail. Panama City, Panama, here I come. That trip was a defining moment in my life. Being on that beach, feeling the ocean breeze, sounds of the waves hitting shore, smell of the water, I couldn't believe I was in Panama. While writing this, I'm looking at pictures of a sunrise that I took while I was there. I had them enlarged, printed, and framed. I remember being so at peace and just grateful for the opportunity to be able to be in God's grace. Grateful to my friend for inviting me. It was a once in a lifetime experience, many people don't get.

I'm sure there are several reasons that can be attributed to why people find it hard to travel. Perhaps out of fear, finances, the right time, no one to go with, or any number of other reasons. I am forever blessed that I was able to go. I decided, after that trip, I want to go somewhere new every year. I have a passport, and it needs to be used. From that moment on, I made it a point to go somewhere different each year. I have been to Panama, Costa Rica, Dubai, Egypt, Ghana, and my most recent international trip, November 2024, the Dominican Republic. This was a special trip for me because it was a solo trip. I had always wanted to do a solo trip and for my birthday, I shocked myself and booked the trip. I fearfully did it. I couldn't believe I made that happen. Truly one of the most liberating experiences I've ever had. I was able to become closer with God. I didn't have to wait for anybody. I was on my own time. I did the activities that I wanted to do, ate the food that I wanted to eat, met new people and was able to sit back and just observe everything and everyone around me. Traveling to different countries, states, cities, and experiencing different cultures has made me appreciate where I come from even more. Also, traveling created some of the most immersive, educational experiences I have had in life. I love the opportunity to get out and have new adventures while conquering fear head on. DO IT SCARED, RIGHT?

I am not a fan of heights at all, especially bridges, but I love to fly. While in Costa Rica we were going on a hike through

Miravalles Volcano, with an elevation of over 6,000 feet. Beautiful scenery. Our tour guide warned us about some trails and suspended bridges. Of course, panic set in. There was a suspended bridge that led to a waterfall. The second I saw it, I wanted to run the other way, and I'm not a runner. This thing was so far in the air, and it was swinging. Thank GOD for cheerleaders. My friends sure did know how to convince me to go for it. I just had to pray the whole way across, burning hands, from gripping the sides of the bridge so tightly, sweat dripping down my face, and a sense of urgency behind me. I didn't get a chance to really take in the scenery because I was too scared of being exposed that high up. What kept me going was my friend behind me cheering me on knowing I have this fear. I kept moving forward, one foot in front of the other. Once across the bridge, there was the most magnificent sight, a waterfall, with a vibrant, illuminating rainbow, which made it all worth it. Then reality set in, there was only one way back to our tractor that brought us to the volcano, the way we came. OH NO, but we made it! I am so grateful for the cheerleaders I have in my life. Their support encourages me to get out of my comfort zone and experience things I didn't think were possible.

REFLECTION

Find a reason to put life into living, because life is meant to be experienced, not for you to just exist. Living day to day can be scary and finding how you can add meaning to life can be frustrating, especially if you feel like you don't have the means. I want to encourage you to think about what you like. Think about what you don't like. Try to look at what you do every day, whether it's work, school, taking care of family, your health, or finances and see where you can add more life to just your regular everyday routine. If you want to take a trip somewhere, plan it out. If it's someplace you want to go, I don't care if it takes a year. TAKE ACTION, ORGANIZE, AND SCHEDULE IT! Face it, nothing is cheap nowadays and it's a struggle just to meet basic needs, but I want you to know that it's okay to think about yourself sometimes, even if it's just a day trip to the park or taking the kids to a movie. There are some hidden gems just in your own backyard, your own city, state, and country. You don't have to go far to have new adventures and experiences.

- Walk a trail that you've never walked
- Listen to some music that you've never entertained, pay attention to the lyrics, not just the melody.
- Sit by the ocean and just listen to the waves on a cloudy day.
- During a rainstorm, shut off your TV, put away your phone, turn off the music and just listen to the droplets hit the window, hit the roof. Listen to the sound of the thunder and see how that makes you feel.

- And if you haven't, try to be a tourist in your own City. I know there are plenty of places in my city

- that I know nothing about, have never done, have never experienced, and I'm looking forward to doing that. I want you to do the same.

Some things I want you to ask yourself as you're trying to find things that bring you Joy:

- Do you feel calm?
- Do you feel more alive?
- Do you feel anxious?

Let me share a couple of my favorite quotes about life that may help ENCOURAGE YOU!

Live as if you were to die tomorrow learn as if you were to live forever -Mahatma Gandhi

To live is to suffer to survive is to find some meaning in the suffering -Friedrich Nietzsche

Chapter 4

Never Give Up on You

Never giving up means continuing to strive towards your goal or your objective. Even in the face of difficulties, setbacks, or challenges, it puts emphasis on perseverance, resilience, and determination. Never giving up encourages individuals to stay focused and keep trying even when things seem tough. According to the Merriam-Webster Dictionary, Perseverance is continued effort to do or achieve something, despite difficulties, failure, or opposition. Resilience is an ability to recover from, or adjust easily to, misfortune or change. Determination is the act of deciding definitively and firmly; or the fixed intention to achieve a desired end. Never giving up is a mindset. It is an internal struggle for some people to have the belief that they can achieve in life, especially when they have outside influences telling them that they cannot. Society is consumed with everybody else's opinions on what acceptance should look like, what you should say, what you should wear, what you should eat, and how you should feel about certain topics. Those influencing opinions and views, skew and alter, personal judgment, rendering many people incapable of thinking and acting on their own behalf. So many people are afraid to go against the crowd, afraid to step out on their own, because they may be judged for it. The most important thing to know is that at the end of the day, YOU must be happy with YOU! It's so important for people to realize that their own happiness can't come from any outside resources. Only you can truly make yourself happy. Understanding and believing that is where true JOY resides. When people continue to hinge their happiness on other people, circumstances, or things, once that's taken away, so is that happiness. You know what else gets taken away? Motivation to pour into self. Pouring into self is the most important factor in helping others.

I decided years ago that the most important tool I had, to help me to continue to fight this disease every day, was to pour into me as much as possible. Meaning even on the hardest days, I had to show up for myself. One of the ways that I continue to show up for myself is being active. Having a disease that can progress at any time due to any number of factors, infections, medications no longer working, or stress, I know that I need to stay as active as possible. I had to change the foods and drinks that I consume. Increasing my level of activity has been a tremendous help in keeping my mobility. Living a sedentary lifestyle is a quick way to end up immobile. Stress is the number one cause for flare-ups and relapses for me, so I've learned to set boundaries when it comes to the people that I interact with and activities that I participate in.

I was recently a participant in a fundraising walk, WalkMS, for Multiple Sclerosis awareness a couple of weeks ago, and even more elated when a few of my family and friends also participated in the walk. I am thankful and grateful to have the ability to use my limbs. There were many other MS Warriors that participated who had their walkers, their canes, and their wheelchairs. Having an assistive device isn't shameful and it doesn't diminish who they are, or who we are. Each of us has our own cross to bear, whether visible or invisible. No one would ever know I have MS if I didn't tell them. Before that walk of three miles, earlier that morning I had also participated in a fitness class. I told myself hey I've got the energy I'm still going to do this walk; besides, I've got people showing up for me and I need to show up for myself. At the end of those 3 miles, I realized that I had pushed myself to the max. But I was so happy to have completed it and made it to the finish line. I ended up in bed for the next 24 hours but sometimes it's about celebrating the small victories that keep me going.

Even 1% better each day is better than doing nothing. Over the years I have tried many different activities so I wouldn't get bored and discouraged. Giving up is not an option. I've tried boxing, CrossFit, walking trails, going to the gym, and even classes such as yoga, Zumba, and step board just to name a few. All these different activities have kept me going because I was able to change it up. I wasn't afraid to be the newbie in a room full of strangers. Sure, I knew I'd be in a new environment with new people. The introvert in me did not let that deter me. The number one thing I do each day is choose to focus on how to become better and stronger physically, mentally, and spiritually. I do my best to proceed without any judgments. I don't focus on whether I'm being judged because I must show up for myself and not give up.

REFLECTION

Perseverance, Resilience, and Determination are key components in progressing in life. Showing up for yourself will help you to show up for others. On a plane, in case of emergency, they don't tell you to put your oxygen mask on first for no reason. If you pass out, how can you possibly be present to help another in need? Being optimistic in the face of adversity can be a powerful tool. DO NOT GIVE UP on yourself. No one is going to treat you better than you treat yourself. Optimism can help you push through, especially when you have a goal in mind, no matter how small. For instance, take that old saying about the glass being half empty or half full, those who see the glass as half full would be seen as an optimist, those who see the glass as half empty would be considered a pessimist. In all actuality, people should just be happy to have the glass in the first place. As long as you have the glass, you're able to pour into it what you want to get out of it. The more positivity you pour into it, the more positivity you're able to pour into others. Some ways for you to incorporate more positivity:

- FOCUS on your needs whenever possible even if that means eating a meal, taking a shower, ignoring that phone call, or adjusting your sleep schedule. Nurturing your immediate needs recharge YOU! So, on those days when you want to give up on yourself, DON'T!

- REFLECT on how far you have come. You are not the same person you were 1 year ago, 5 years ago, 10 years ago. You are not even the same person you were a month ago and that is something you can applaud.

- CONGRATULATE and REWARD yourself every step of the way. Be proud of yourself for even the most minute change towards improvement. Each step adds up. Remember it is PROGRESS NOT PREFECTION we seek!

Chapter 5

Learn to Listen to Your Body

Two big L words LISTEN and LEARN. To learn, is to gain knowledge or understanding of a skill, a study, instruction, or experience. To listen, means to pay attention to; be alert; to catch an unexpected sound. Listening isn't always just about hearing a sound. Like the definition says, it means to pay attention, to be alert, to give consideration. Often people don't listen to their bodies. They push themselves every day. We've normalized hustle culture so much that it's always, go go go. The world is set up for constant movement, rarely for being still. Being still allows us to focus on what's going on physically, mentally, emotionally, and spiritually within us. Recognizing changes in those areas is vital because they are intertwined with one another. If all those areas are not nourished and cohesive, this makes everyday tasks more difficult for us to complete, and we don't even realize. It's so hard for people to understand what they pay attention to:

- The physical signs our bodies give us
- When we are around certain people

- Conversations we engage in
- What we put into our bodies
- What we constantly listen to
- What we see on the news
- What we read on social media platforms

is paramount in understanding why symptoms manifest in the first place. All these situations and circumstances heavily affect us physically, emotionally, mentally, and spiritually, even if it is not directly happening to us at that moment. Recognizing when this is occurring will help center us and reroute us back to where we need to be, if that's what you want.

I remember a time when my hands first locked up. I was writing a lot that day. I got so scared because I didn't know what to do. It never happened to me before and my fingers were just stuck in this contorted position. I couldn't move and I was almost on the verge of tears because of the pain. I was freaking out and I was thinking oh my God is this the way my hands are going to be for the rest of my life? Am I going to need somebody to help me feed myself? Am I going to be unable to wipe myself in the bathroom? At that moment I had to exhale! I had to relax and after a few minutes my fingers went back to their natural state. Now mind you my hands have been numb for 14 years, that is not going away. I still have the ability to use my hands and fingers. I try to do strength training by using the occupational therapy tools that I was given, as well as exercises with my hands to help with my coordination and build strength. I will admit, I do not do them as often as I should. Simple tasks such as buttoning a top or tying my shoes can be somewhat difficult. There have been several occasions when my hands locked up again. I remember if I relax, and do not focus so much on the problem, it will eventually fix itself. This is also a sign I need to rest. It's a cue that I could not do any more typing or writing that day. I've learned over the years that this is the process I need to go through each time it happens.

I used to draw when I was younger, especially sketches of people. I really miss that aspect of my life. It was about to be my 10-year anniversary of having MS, and I decided I wanted a new tattoo. I wanted it to be something that I created. Something that was a symbol of my MS and my faith. I knew it was going to take some time. Not just hours but maybe a day or two. Mentally and physically, I had to prepare myself for my hands to lock up, to be in excruciating pain, plus the stinging sensation, but I was willing to endure that because this is something that I wanted to do for myself. I didn't want to pay for somebody else to draw a design for me. It took me a few days to draw those tattoos though. I was so proud of myself for finishing. Yes, my hands were cramped up, they locked up, and I had to take several breaks, but the result was beautiful. I'm just happy I was able to listen to my body through the entire process.

REFLECTION

Have you ever paid attention to your body, especially how it reacts to certain people or certain situations? What do you do to remove yourself from the situation? Do you overthink in that situation? I've found the best way to eliminate that physical strain, to reduce the emotional reaction, or that mental anguish, is to listen to your body.

- Focus on your breathing at that moment.
- Pay attention to the thoughts that you're having at that moment.
- Recognize what parts of your body are being affected.
- Sometimes it's best to remove yourself from the situation all together and leave.

Allowing yourself time to regroup and gather Your thoughts are healing processes.

Oftentimes, I turn to scripture. I follow a lesson plan, or I utilize several different versions of bible scriptures to help me interpret the message I am supposed to receive from the passage. The messages received also stem from how strong my relationship is with the Most High. Discussing different passages with friends, with a pastor, or bible study group, when you feel trauma triggers from life's obstacles is a great way to explore alternative perspectives to gain a stronger spiritual connection. When physical symptoms arise, don't be afraid to reach out to your doctor at the slightest hint of change in your body, because that could be the key to preventing your symptoms from getting worse.

These suggestions are not just for those with a chronic illness or disorder. These strategies can be utilized for anyone suffering with their own internal struggles having to do with an addiction, mental health issues, family problems, relationship problems, or medical issues. The key is to recognize what triggers negative responses and reduce STRESS, so that YOU can take control, and increase a POSITIVE outcome. Stress is a silent killer, so don't take for granted the importance of reducing your stress levels as much as possible. Understand that everyday life brings its own stressors, but it's up to you to be able to choose how long you allow that stress to affect you!

Chapter 6

Don't Allow Others to Tell You How You Feel

To feel, can be attributed or synonymous to our sense of touch, or to perceive by a physical sensation; To handle or touch to examine, test, or explore some quality. It is to be conscious of an inward impression, state of mind, or physical condition. I'm sure there are plenty of times where you just were not up to going out with friends, going to that party, clocking into work, taking your child to football, basketball, soccer practice, dance recitals, gymnastics, or even cooking dinner. It seemed to be the most impossible task in the world some days. People around us can talk us into doing things that we just don't feel like doing. Just don't have the energy to do it or just don't have the time to do it. It's important to realize that when you don't feel like doing something due to motivation or physical limitation, it can cause us to complete the task or engage in the activity without being 100% present. It's hard for people to recognize that their feelings are valid, especially when they don't want to let anybody down. When we're doing something that we just don't have the energy or motivation to do; it's going to cause us to dread doing it again. Feelings are completely subjective and no one person can tell any individual how they feel. Not in a moment, not when engaging in an activity, not during a conversation, or in the process of completing certain activities. It is important to have the CONFIDENCE to ADVOCATE for yourself when there is no one else to speak up for you, otherwise people will take advantage when and where they can. Nobody likes being exploited.

Many times, throughout my life that I have allowed other people to tell me how I should feel regarding something, pertaining to what was said, something that I heard, something that I saw. Sure, it made me question myself instead of trusting myself more. Being an overthinker, I would always replay the scenario repeatedly. Feel guilt, feel shame, or feel resentment towards the individual or individuals. You know that familiar saying, Trust your own GUT! Great advice!

I currently must do injections every 14 days to help manage my disease to keep it stable. There is no cure there or reversal of the damage that's already been done to my brain, spine, or the body parts that are affected. Of course there are side effects to any medication that you take. With this interferon injection, Plegridy, you get flu-like symptoms, body aches, chills, headache, and weakness. This medication is an improvement. When I was first diagnosed, I was on a medication called Rebif where I had to inject myself 3 days a week. The following day after those injections I would still get those flu-like symptoms. I was miserable. I was always exhausted. All I wanted to do was lay in bed. I was too tired. I felt sick all the time and the medication that was supposed to keep me stabilized was making me feel even worse. Multiple Sclerosis is monitored by MRI. In the beginning stages, I got MRIs every 6 months. A change in scan, showing more damage, or a new lesion, meant my neurologist would recommend switching medications. An MRI years ago showed new lesions on my brain and spine, which prompted the conversation about changing medications. I have between 6 and 7 lesions now on my brain and spine. The disease was progressing, and they call that a relapse, hence why I'm now currently on the Plegridy. I was grateful to change to the Plegridy because I no longer had to inject myself 3 days a week. I only had to do it every 14 days, what a relief!

I like to travel, so when I was getting used to doing my injections, I would have to plan it around my injection days. If I knew I was going to be out of town for an injection weekend, I knew I needed to leave the day after, especially if I was driving. The time of day also matters so I would do it later in the evening. Midday I would start feeling the side effects. Feeling horrible and miserable. I was cranky and disconnected. The people around me didn't really understand the magnitude or the amount of energy it took for me to be there for and with them. I wanted to participate but couldn't. They would try to convince me to stay longer. I, knowing what the side effects were, and the effect it had on me mentally and physically, would go against my better judgement to please them. Sometimes it was worth the suffering, other times I wish I would've stayed home, knowing the side effects are going to be horrible. Driving or flying while experiencing these symptoms, intensified the pain for me. I tried to explain it, but nobody really listens. Hearing and listening to a person are two completely different actions. Over the years I became frustrated and tired of repeating myself. I sounded like a broken record. I just stopped and was firm with my boundaries. People really won't understand until they actually get it. I would never want somebody to experience what I experience daily.

REFLECTION

So, Warriors out there, I want you to know that it is okay to speak up for yourself. It is okay to be an advocate for your health. For your mental health, your physical health, and your emotional health. You can accomplish this by:

- Being firm about your time management
- Be open to alternative ways to enjoy the company of others
- Educate them about how you're feeling, invite and open dialogue.

Hopefully they'll be willing to listen to you and recognize when you're just having a hard day. Everybody likes to be invited, yet sometimes you just can't participate and that's okay. What you should focus on is studying your own patterns.

Ask yourself:

- Why are you feeling the way that you're feeling?
- What's the motivating factor in taking part in the activity in question?
- Why would you continue to participate if it's not something you find fulfilling?

When you know your WHY, it gives you a sense of clarity about who you are. The most POWERFUL thing you can do, is to KNOW who you are! God will honor your WHY. Be sure that your motive behind that WHY is pure. Once you figure that out, NO ONE can stop YOU! Do not forget to put YOURSELF first a bit more. You are balancing so much already. You are handling things nobody sees or understands. I know you are doing your best and trying harder than anybody can imagine. CULTIVATE, FEEL and SHOW up for YOU! On the hardest days, REST! IT'S PRICELESS!

Chapter 7

Rebound from Relapses

When I hear the word rebound, I automatically think about basketball and how the ball bounces off the backboard after a missed shot. The player tries to catch it so they can attempt to make the basket again. Rebounds are a powerful thing. Points add up, possibly leading to a victory at the end of the game. The goal is to win, right? The ability to rebound means to recover from a setback, or frustration, or to spring back from a collision or impact with another body. It can also mean upward or movement in general. Rebounding in everyday life is so crucial to moving forward, to growth, and to success. Who doesn't want to succeed in life? To succeed, we must learn to rebound from life's failures, missed shots, or obstacles. What a difficult concept this is, especially for those who find themselves stuck in a low place, that valley, looking up at the mountain, and how far it is to climb. Pending doom sets in, repeating that failure again. Not realizing, as YOU keep climbing and slipping back down, YOU are getting stronger each time, going a little bit higher. Until finally reaching the top.

Relapses can occur in any aspect of life. Whether it be a relapse for a medical illness. A relapse from an addiction. A relapse from a toxic relationship. People experience relapses every day, depending on what series of events are happening in their life, at any given time. We don't know what each of us is going through. We don't know what each of us needs to rebound from. It's important to allow some Grace.

God GIVES us Grace without judgement. My last relapse was in 2020. We all know what happened in 2020. A horrible pandemic shut us down. Shut the world down. I had so much hope that year. I was going to be turning 40 later that year. I was excited about going on another international trip, my first cruise. Then our worlds were turned upside down. I worked for a few months and then was eventually laid off in May of 2020. I was faced with not only being confined to my home, only leaving for necessities, but I had no job. My panic and anxiety levels were high. Constantly asking myself, what am I going to do? How am I going to make it? How am I going to survive? I've been working since I was 17 years old, and this is the first time that I've ever been unemployed for longer than a month. So, I did what I wanted to do to keep myself entertained. I DRANK.

Thinking back, I have to say, I was doing WAY TOO MUCH. I was making trays of Jello shots, perfecting my recipes. Wine, bourbon, whiskey, you name it. It was ridiculous! Even that became boring after a while. I had to check my own behavior and make a change.

I was out of work for 9 months before I accepted a position with a great company. I was getting invited for virtual interviews during my job search, but God told me not to settle for anything less than what I was asking for. God made a way for all of my needs to be met, and bills paid. I listened to Him. He told me to listen to my body. God knew what was coming and knew I needed that rest and time to reflect. I considered this unemployment trial as an opportunity. An opportunity to prepare and be satisfied with where I was in life at that moment. I took time to express JOY. Troubles have a way of making you grow stronger.

Towards the end of 2020, in December, I noticed numbness and pain increasing on the right side of my body. I knew that something was wrong, and I had no choice but to go see my doctor, even though I did not want to be in anybody's hospital setting during the pandemic. When I called to set up an appointment, I was devastated to find out that my neurologist of 10 years was forced to retire due to being over 70 years old.

They considered her high risk for contracting COVID. I had to see a new provider. Tell them all about my history. I was frustrated and I did not trust anyone. They recommended an inpatient hospital stay for three days but I refused. With a compromised immune system already, and no definitive answers as to what was going on with COVID, I just couldn't allow them to admit me to the hospital. I looked at my doctor and I asked her what's my alternative? My new neurologist told me my alternative was to take a high dosage of steroids at home. This meant I had to take 25 pills a day. I said anything is better than being admitted to the hospital. Why? I was fearful I would never leave the hospital again, with so many unknowns about this new disease, I did not want to take any more unnecessary risks.

My faith in God is what got me through. Having a weak faith, or a suppressed faith, can blind us to God. God SHOWS and God SPEAKS; you just must be STILL and LISTEN. I had to say Lord, whatever your will for me, EMPOWER me to do it! I no longer doubt God when I ask God for something. My faith is in Him alone. I truly believe God hears, He listens. He responds in His own way, and in His own time. The blessing of being laid off from work, being able to take care of all my needs during those entire 9 months, was His preparation for me to endure this relapse. He knew I needed all the STRENGTH I had, to

OVERCOME and to REBOUND from that relapse. God has a reason for doing everything and I do not question Him.

Doubt causes us to wonder whether our interactions with God are real or possible. Pay attention to the signs. He'll answer you. God answers through a kind word from a stranger. God answers through the wind. God answers through a rainstorm. Seeing a cardinal in a tree. A street sign. A license plate. A song. He does answer, we just must learn to pay attention.

REFLECTION

What blessings has God bestowed upon you that you didn't even realize was a blessing at the time? I live by the creed DELAYED NOT DENIED. Sometimes things don't need to happen at the time that we wanted. It needs to happen at the time that you're ready to receive it. Have FAITH that it will happen just make sure you are prepared when He comes through!

- Faith in Him, enables us to receive God's blessing
- Faith empowers us to recognize His blessings
- Faith encourages us to look beyond what we see
- Faith challenges us to bless God and to give Him thanks during the waiting period

When we ask God for something, God might say yes. God might say no. God might say later. Ask yourself if you're prepared to hear NO? When that RELAPSE occurs (whatever that looks like for you), some actions/activities that may help you REBOUND could look like:

- Having a spa day
- Exploring a hobby, something that you've never tried before but found interesting
- Learning about a subject and mastering the subject
- Choosing a friend that you haven't spoken to in a long time reaching out to them. Invite them out for lunch just to catch up
- Or just a simple phone call to hear their voice let them know that you're thinking about them. A kind word goes a long way.

I recommend you try some of these activities out and see how you feel in a week, or in a month.

Chapter 8

Learn the Art of the Slow Yes and the Quick No

This concept was presented to me through a book by Greg McKeown called *Essentialism: The Disciplined Pursuit of Less*. We are so accustomed to saying yes to our family, friends, partners, coworkers, and kids, without even considering if we want to do it. We do it out of obligation. We do it out of guilt. When we don't want to do it at all, or at least would have appreciated some time to think about it before actually making that decision. Before you know it, you've already said yes, and you don't want to take it back or disappoint the person that asked. Why is it so hard to say no? NO is a complete sentence! Saying no without an explanation should also be normalized. People have become so accustomed to questioning why people do the things that they do, say the things that they say, without just allowing that person to be who they are. Personally, I used to say yes, all the time to people. I was a yes person because I was a people pleaser. I didn't want to let anybody down. I felt guilty whenever I said no. They would often try to make me feel guilty for saying no so I'd give in. Those times I would just say yes so, they would stop asking, but when it came time to do what was being asked of me, I resented it and sometimes regretted it. There were occasions when I was glad that I said yes, due to enjoying the experiences, even though I didn't want to. Then it hit me. During this chronic illness era of my life, I realized no one can make you do anything you do not want to do. Instead of committing immediately, it's okay to pause and take a beat. It's okay to give that quick no. It's also okay to think about it and give a slow yes. I had to tell myself this repeatedly until it finally resonated with me that NO is a complete sentence. I didn't have to explain myself to anyone, especially when the explanation was not going to change that person's perception of the situation. And if you remember in the previous chapter, when I asked, are you prepared to hear NO, I also had to ask myself the same thing. Would I be able to handle being told no. Who likes to be told no? Understanding why the NO was given, without forcing the other individual to explain themselves, is one of the simplest acts of understanding. This is where true GRACE plays a vital role.

REFLECTION

Being alone can be scary, especially if you don't find comfort in your own company. You may be a person who says yes to everything because you're afraid that when you need someone, they're going to tell you no because you told them no. When doing something for someone, we must reevaluate our motives for doing it. You shouldn't do things for the accolades or for something in return. Do it because you want to. When practicing the art of the slow yes and the quick no, I want you to make a conscious informed decision. Sure, it is wonderful to want to help occasionally. However, take into consideration what things YOU need to accomplish before helping that person.

- When it comes to a coworker, have you met that deadline that you needed to meet?
- When it comes to helping a family member, have you taken care of your needs first?
- Have you considered everything that goes into what's required to accomplish what that person asked you to do?
- Are you going to have the time?
- Are you going to have the energy?
- Are you going to do it with a positive attitude?
- Are you doing it out of an ulterior motive?

Ask yourself these questions before committing to YES! Learn to embrace GRACE for yourself and for others. More importantly, allow the reception of GRACE extended to YOU, by others. YOU DESERVE GRACE TOO! And remember, NO IS A COMPLETE SENTENCE!

Chapter 9

Realize You're not Limited

You only have Limitations

A limit is something that bounds, restrains, or confines. We experience limits every day. For example, a speed limit, and a limit to how much alcohol you can consume before you're deemed intoxicated. The amount of money withdrawn from an ATM. How many items you are allowed to purchase at a store during a sale. These limits differ from limits pertaining to the inability to physically do something. Showing up in your everyday life and completing a simple task, such as taking a bath, washing your hair, doing your nails, walking to the bus stop, singing a song, reading that street sign two blocks away, or focusing on the book that's in your hand is normal right? However, with a new physical limitation, those everyday things are not as simple to complete. Things you used to do, without thinking about it, can seem impossible. People may feel embarrassed, humiliated, or frustrated. DEFEATED! How can you gain confidence and maintain independence when you are in a reality of inability? By rerouting your mind to think about alternative ways to do tasks. THINK OUTSIDE OF THE BOX!

Honestly, the first decade living with my chronic illness was a learning experience. Very early, while navigating life with my symptoms, I remembered one incident where I was in my kitchen. I grabbed a bottle of cold water out of the fridge, and with these numb hands and tiny fingers, I tried to twist the cap off the bottle. Surprisingly enough this was a problem. I had opened thousands of bottles with my hands before. Never thought about having to struggle to open a simple bottle of water until I was standing alone in my home. I could not do it no matter how hard I tried. I could not get that bottle open. I was livid. I was thirsty. I was tired. I was DEFEATED! I was so upset I wanted to cry and I am quite sure a tear did fall down my face. But do you know what I did? I said to myself hmm what other tools or abilities do I have that can assist me? I stuck the top of that bottle in between my teeth, and I twisted that bottle cap off. Granted that's not something I want to do in public, for fear of people looking at me strangely but you got to do what you got to do is what I say. That is the day I embraced the notion I am NOT LIMITED I JUST HAVE LIMITATIONS. I knew I needed to find other ways to ADAPT. How did I make life easier for myself? I found tools, equipment, and strategies that would assist me in being successful. For instance, easy twist off caps for medications. When it comes to opening jars, I have a kitchen aid that helps to grip the top of the jar so that I can twist it off. When walking, sometimes my legs are so weak and swollen that I must wear braces to help reduce the swelling. Now I will use adaptive equipment whenever I need it. I had removed the thought of embarrassment. Telling myself that I am not less of a human being because I needed assistance. If it will help me maintain my independence, I welcome the aid. When I need help, I'm not as afraid to ask. The things that I can do I do. The things that I cannot do I either figure out a way that allows me to accomplish them, or I ask someone else to do it for me or at least assist. I laugh because in retrospect, instead of using my teeth to open that bottle, I could've just gone to my kitchen faucet and filled a cup up with water, if I was that thirsty, but that would've been too easy.

REFLECTION

My dear Warrior, the secret is to not allow the fact that you can't do everything, keep you from doing something. Pace yourself. Do an activity, then rest. Always rest when you get overwhelmed. Whether you need to run, walk, or crawl, the most important thing for you to do is to keep going until you can't go anymore.

Do not be afraid of limitations. So what if you don't succeed the first time.

- TRY AGAIN! IF you cannot do it at that moment, STOP! No need aggravating yourself and exhausting more energy.
- REDUCE the STRESS that this moment of inability is creating for you.
- PAUSE whatever you're doing, take a DEEP BREATH, and FOCUS your thoughts.
- PROCESS your emotions. How do you feel? What's going on with your body physically? Then proceed with intention.

Chapter 10

Refuse to Sink

To REFUSE is to be unwilling to accept or comply with. To REFUSE is to not allow someone to have or to deny. To SINK means to go to the bottom, to submerge, to become partly buried, to become engulfed, or to fall or drop to a lower place or level. REFUSING to SINK means you're unwilling to become engulfed, consumed, or buried in that lower place. When in a dark place, it can be hard to find your way out with no light guiding you. Yet FAITH is believing in something you cannot see. Why is having blind faith so hard for people? Most people only believe what they can see, hear, touch, taste, or feel. When consumed with darkness you must believe that you're going to make it out. This requires TRUST and being VULNERABLE.

Every day I wake up, it's a struggle just to get out of bed. I'm always tired. Fatigue is my biggest symptom with this disease. I'm always in pain and about 2 years ago I started noticing rashes and breakouts on my skin. I didn't know what was going on. I had to go see a dermatologist who told me, sometimes people with

Multiple Sclerosis develop other autoimmune disorders which in my case was eczema. I grew up with very sensitive skin and couldn't wear certain perfumes or lotions. As an adult, I was able to incorporate those things. With the eczema diagnosis, I have not one, but two autoimmune disorders. Fast forward maybe 6 months, my hair starts falling out in patches. I didn't think anything of it at first when I saw the first patch, and then more and more hair started falling out. Most of my hair had fallen out within probably a month. Here comes another diagnosis, Alopecia Areata. BOOM, 3 autoimmune disorders. Multiple Sclerosis, Eczema, and Alopecia Areata. I have an unusually high pain tolerance, but steroid shots in my scalp were excruciating. My dermatologist did about 15 injections every 4 weeks to help stimulate hair growth. At that point, I was willing to do anything.

The walls just felt like they were closing in on me. My whole identity was changing, and I felt I had no control. The hardest part was knowing that it was my own body working against me. I started questioning what I did to deserve this? Why is this happening to me again? How can I fix this? I had to sit with myself and come to terms that all those things, losing my hair and the skin breakouts, wasn't the end of the world. I felt like I was just sinking, defeated from within. My body is rejecting me. It's me against me, every day. It was hard enough fighting one disease let alone three and all I could do was pray and talk to God. This is another storm that God knew he would help see me through, another way for me to strengthen my faith in Him.

I witnessed a dear friend, and mother figure, fighting the same disease as I. She was diagnosed with Multiple Sclerosis around the same time I was diagnosed. Within 10 years, her fight ended. One of the strongest people I have ever met. I admire the way she showed up for herself when she could. She is the one person who REFUSED TO SINK. Her progressive form was too much for her body to handle. I admit it was scary watching her go through her symptoms while experiencing my own symptoms. The progressive form advances more quickly. Here I am, with the relapsing remitting form, knowing there is a strong possibility it can advance to the progressive form. I felt like I was facing my own mortality, while watching her fight her own battle. But everyone's diagnosis, treatments, and outcomes are not the same. Everyone's experience with chronic illness is different. Everyone's life experience is different. She is my motivating force to keep fighting every day even when I do not want to fight.

When you see a ship what comes to mind? I think about an anchor and how it allows the ship to stay in one place until that anchor is lifted. Almost like a root from a tree. I think about being rooted in my faith. My faith is what keeps me afloat and being anchored in that faith, while in that boat, I'm supposed to be still and listen to what God is trying to tell me. Through this trial. Through this tribulation. Through this challenge. I know that there is a blessing within. God is preparing me for what is next. One of the tattoos I mentioned in chapter 5, Learn to Listen to Your Body, is a picture of an anchor with a ribbon around it that says I REFUSE TO SINK!

REFLECTION

He is not going to let you sink. With His help and guidance, YOU can REFUSE TO SINK. In Philippians 4: 10-14 I rejoiced in the Lord greatly, now at length you have revived your concern for me; indeed, you were concerned before but lacked opportunity. Not that I speak from want, for I have learned to be content in whatever circumstance I am. I know how to get along with humble means, and I also know how to live prosperity; in any and every circumstance I have learned the secret of being filled and going hungry, both having abundance and suffering need. I can do all things through Him who STRENGTHENS me. Nevertheless, you have done well to share with me my affliction."

God has a purpose for us all. Remember your purpose is not for everyone, and you can't make your purpose be someone else's purpose. I want you to realize that purpose is about destiny, not about human desire. Everyone is fighting a battle none of us knows about. However, do not diminish your circumstance or situation, at the sacrifice of your own healing.

Closing Reflections

Final Thoughts: From My Heart to Yours

I wrote *Embracing the MonSter Within* not because I had all the answers, but because I had a story—and I knew that story might just be the lifeline someone else needed. This book was born from pain, yes, but also from perseverance, faith, stubborn hope, and a sprinkle of humor (because if you can't laugh at your symptoms occasionally, are you even coping?).

This book matters because chronic illness is often invisible, misunderstood, and isolating—but you don't have to navigate it alone. Whether you're battling MS, another condition, or just the overwhelming weight of being human in a broken world, I want you to know you are not alone, and your struggle is not small.

I hope you leave these pages with more than information—I hope you leave with **PERMISSION**. Permission to rest. To rage. To believe in healing. To cry in the shower and then get up and keep going. I want you to walk away knowing you are worthy, even on your messiest, most fatigued, can't-feel-my-legs kind of day.

Writing this book changed me. It peeled back layers I didn't know I was hiding behind. It reminded me that being vulnerable is not weakness, it's holy. And it gave me back pieces of myself this illness tried to steal.

Here's my call to action: Speak up. Love hard. Let go of shame. Take a nap. Demand better care. Show up as you are, not who the world expects you to be. Be the warrior and the healer, the soft heart and the steel spine. You don't have to choose.

If this is the only page you read, let me pour this into your spirit: You are not broken. You are becoming. And God is not finished with you yet.

Final Message:
This isn't the end—it's a spark. Keep rising, keep laughing, keep believing. Your story is far from over, and the world needs your fire.

Discussion Questions

The life you've been dreaming of is on the other side of fear. What are your deepest fears?

What would you do if you weren't afraid?

Being BRAVE doesn't mean you are not scared, it means doing it scared anyway. What does being BRAVE look like to you?

In what ways have you PERSEVERED through STRENGTH that no one knows about? How does this make you feel?

Who or what has been your biggest support and what does that person or thing do to make you feel supported?

What are some situations, things, or even people, that make you feel bad about yourself in life? If you had the courage, what would you do or say in that situation?

What is something you have always wanted to do but thought you'd never be able to do?

What does living your life to the fullest look like for you?

What actions can you take to help you achieve that?

What are 3 small, yet significant changes you can make to take care of yourself and support others?

Imagine your perfect day. Describe it in as much detail as possible, including who you are with and what you are doing. How does this image make you feel?

Tools for Success:

I want you to write a letter to your future self, whether it is 3 months from now, 6 months from now, or 12 months from now. Think about your answers above and make a goal to execute what you said. If your deadline happens to be the end of the year, plan to read it on December 31st, to reflect on all the things you've accomplished.

Create a Vision Board or a Vision Board Journal. Place on it what you want to see manifest in your life. This can be short term or long term. When you see the vision, you can make it happen!

About the Author

Kinyotta was born and raised in St. Louis, Missouri, where her passion for helping others was ignited at an early age. With nearly 25 years of experience in healthcare, she has dedicated her life to service, care, and making a lasting impact on the lives of those she touches. A global traveler with an adventurous spirit, Kinyotta finds inspiration in the diverse people and places she encounters around the world.

Her debut book, *Embracing the MonSter Within: 10 Strategies on Navigating a Chronic Illness through Strength and Perseverance*, is a deeply personal work inspired by her 14-year journey with Multiple Sclerosis. Despite the struggles, Kinyotta has successfully slowed the disease's progression and written this book to empower others facing similar battles. Through her words, she offers strength, encouragement, and practical guidance for anyone living with a chronic illness.

Outside of her professional and writing life, Kinyotta is passionate about music, art, and spending time in nature. She especially enjoys capturing the beauty around her through photography—whether it's friends and family, her world travels, or the quiet elegance of the natural world. More recently, she has become an advocate for those suffering from Multiple Sclerosis. Her role as a District Activist Leader, with the Advocacy

Program for the National Multiple Sclerosis Society, is where she hopes to affect policy change for MS Research. She is immensely grateful for the unwavering love and support of those closest to her, who continue to inspire her journey of healing and hope.